TOP 10 TIPS

FOR ENJOYING

SUCCESS IN SCHOOL

SUSAN HENNEBERG

ROSEN
PUBLISHING®

NEW YORK

Thanks to my daughters for their help with this book. They are such inspiring role models for anyone who wants to enjoy success in school, career, and life.

Published in 2013 by The Rosen Publishing Group, Inc.
29 East 21st Street, New York, NY 10010

First Edition

Library of Congress Cataloging-in-Publication Data

Henneberg, Susan.
Top 10 tips for enjoying success in school/Susan Henneberg. — 1st ed.
      p. cm. — (Tips for success)
Includes bibliographical references and index.
ISBN 978-1-4488-6860-5 (library binding)
1. Study skills. 2. Students — Time management. 3. Academic achievement. I. Title.
II. Title: Top ten tips for enjoying success in school.
LB1601.H46 2013
371.30281 — dc23

                                                                                2012003026

Manufactured in the United States of America

CPSIA Compliance Information: Batch #S12YA: For further information, contact Rosen Publishing, New York, New York, at
1-800-237-9932.

CONTENTS

INTRODUCTION

School is a challenging place. As you move from elementary to middle to high school, you have more work. Essays, projects, and lab reports seem more difficult. There is pressure everywhere. Technology such as cell phones, Facebook, instant messaging, and YouTube may seem more appealing than textbooks.

There is no magic to becoming a successful student. The skills and attitudes you need—setting goals, becoming more organized, studying smarter—can be learned by anyone. They are the same skills and attitudes you need for college and work life. Once you learn and practice them, you will find that you are enjoying school. You begin each day prepared to work hard and challenge yourself. Your friends and teachers look forward to your positive attitude. You have fun in and out of class. And you tackle homework and projects without negative stress.

This is the time to make success in school a priority. Make the commitment now to learn effective study skills and change

Doing well in school takes hard work. It pays off in better grades and a brighter future.

any habits that are holding you back. Start by figuring out what you want out of the next few years of your life. Take charge of your schoolwork and your time. Find friends who will motivate and support you. Practice using technology as a tool, not as a distraction. Believe in yourself. The changes you make now will benefit you for the rest of your life.

SET SHORT-TERM AND LONG-TERM GOALS

What would happen if you began a race but didn't know where the finish line was? You would probably run in the wrong direction. You might never make it to the end. That's what it is like to work without goals. Setting short- and long-term goals gives you a direction to work toward. They are the steps to attaining your dreams.

SHORT-TERM GOALS

A short-term goal is one that you can reach in a semester (one marking period or academic term) or less. The beginning of a school year is a great time to set short-term goals. However, you can do it any time you decide you want to achieve something.

Working toward goals can give you direction and motivation. If you have a friend with similar goals, you can support each other to achieve them.

Getting As and Bs in difficult classes, earning a spot on a varsity team, or making new friends are examples of short-term goals. Other short-term goals might be keeping your locker organized or creating a system for remembering your gym clothes.

The first step to achieving a short-term goal is to make a plan. For example, if you want better grades in math you might follow these steps:

- Commit to spending at least an hour a day on math. Spend part of this time reviewing the lesson. Then complete each practice problem.

- Find a study buddy, another student who has a better understanding of math, who can help you with the problems.
- Ask the teacher, tutor, or another adult to explain the difficult homework problems to you.
- After every quiz or test, review how to do the problems you missed.
- Make a list or chart of your quiz and test scores to see if they are improving. That way you will know if your plan is working.

If your goal is to earn a place on a varsity athletic team, create a similar type of plan. Make a commitment to practicing your basketball shots or working out in the batting cage.

LOOKING AHEAD TO COLLEGE

Are you thinking of going to college after you graduate from high school? Most colleges require an entrance exam, either the ACT test or Scholastic Aptitude Test (SAT). These tests measure reading, writing, math, and reasoning skills. Many students begin studying for them in ninth or tenth grade. One way to prepare is to take the Preliminary Scholastic Aptitude Test (PSAT) in tenth or eleventh grade. Another way is to get the SAT vocabulary word and math problem of the day sent to your cell phone. Both test companies offer a lot of helpful suggestions for finding the right college on their Web sites.

LONG-TERM GOALS

Long-term goals, such as graduating from high school and going to college, involve the same kind of planning. Break the long-term goal down into smaller goals. Keep your eye on the long-term goal while working to accomplish the short-term goals. Here's an example:

Long-Term Goal: Go to college
- Small Goal 1: Take challenging classes that prepare you for college.
- Small Goal 2: Save money for college and learn about financial aid options.
- Small Goal 3: Do your homework and go to class.
- Small Goal 4: Get involved in activities at school or in the community.
- Small Goal 5: Finish high school.

Other long-term goals might include winning a music competition, earning your Eagle Scout rank, or saving money for a senior trip. Each goal—no matter how big or small—builds on your previous goals and accomplishments. The most successful people in life have learned how to set goals and celebrate their progress toward them. While they may have setbacks, they don't let temporary failures keep them from pursuing their dreams.

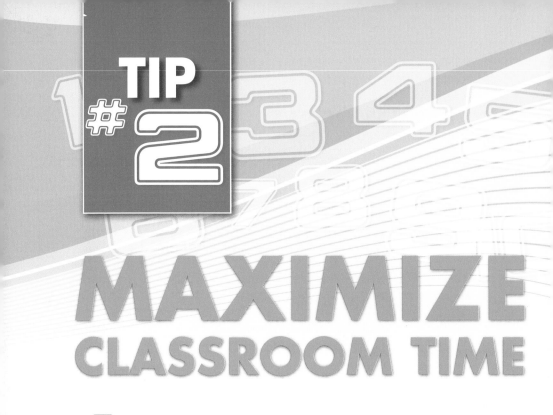

TIP #2

MAXIMIZE CLASSROOM TIME

As a student, you spend most of the school day in the classroom. So it makes sense to maximize this time. You want to take advantage of what the teacher and your classmates can offer you. A bit of preparation, a good attitude, and positive relationships with your teachers can help you make the most of your time in the classroom. Using your personal strengths to your advantage can also help you to learn and succeed.

PREPARATION CAN HELP YOU STAY FOCUSED

A commitment to organization can go a long way in helping you succeed in class. Getting to class on time will be easier if you don't get sidetracked during the passing time in the hallways. If you have taken the time to pack your backpack the night before,

CLUTTER CONTROL FOR LOCKERS

Students often admit that a messy locker makes them late for class. They can't find what they need during the short passing time. A locker shelf can instantly double the amount of storage. Put books for your morning classes on the top shelf. Use the bottom of the locker for books for afternoon classes and after school activities. A peel-and-stick hook on a side of the locker can be handy

An organized locker helps you find what you need quickly. Regular tidying will help it stay that way.

for hanging sports bags or sweatshirts. Finally, a peel-and-stick mirror on the locker door can cut down on hair and makeup checks in the bathroom. Students who take the time to clean out their lockers every Friday will be off to a great start the next Monday.

you will have all the materials you need for each class. If you are late, find out if the homework has already been collected.

Ask your teachers if you can sit near the front. You will stay more engaged with the lesson and will pay more attention. Another way to stay focused is to ask questions and contribute to discussions.

Your teachers may not know you need help unless you ask. Don't be afraid to let them know if you are confused.

Have your planner available to record assignments and due dates. Before you leave the classroom, make sure you know exactly what is expected for the next class.

Here are some other tips that will allow you to get the most out of your classroom time:

- Develop a relationship with your teachers. You want them to see you for who you are, not just the shy kid in the back.
- Write neatly so teachers don't have to struggle to read your writing.
- A mechanical pencil will help you avoid trips to the pencil sharpener.
- If you are confused by a lesson, ask the teacher when might be a good time to discuss it. Don't assume the

"MEAN" TEACHERS

Have you ever had a teacher you thought was mean? She doesn't take late homework. Or she makes you show all your work in math even though you know the answer. Or she doesn't let you sit with your friends. Try looking at this situation from a different point of view. Maybe your teacher just has high expectations for you. She doesn't take late work because she is trying to teach you responsibility. She wants to see your work on math problems to make sure you understand the process. She doesn't let you sit with your friends because they distract you. Remember, teachers choose their profession because they like young people and want them to learn.

teacher has time before or after class. He or she might suggest meeting at lunch or after school.

- If you miss a day because of illness, ask the teacher what you missed instead of a friend. Students may not remember everything important that happened.

Finally, if you have a problem with a teacher, try to resolve it yourself before asking a parent to step in. This shows maturity.

USE YOUR LEARNING STYLE TO YOUR ADVANTAGE

Did you know that your personality style can help you learn? All students have different learning styles. Some students are social learners. They love working on group projects. If this is you, find some study buddies and work on math problems or science projects together. Creative students struggle with routine activities.

A group of students performs a science experiment using a wind tunnel. Many students find that doing hands-on work helps them learn.

They need to find ways to add a unique or original touch to their work. You can add creativity by using different colored pens or pencils. Ask your teacher if you can draw pictures in your notes or create a game as part of a report. Investigative students love to research and solve problems. Their favorite TV show is *History Detectives*. If you are an investigative learner, you can stay engaged by asking questions. Finally, some students learn by doing. They like working on hands-on projects, such as science labs. If this describes you, look for ways to make a model, develop a skit, or do a demonstration for the class as a school activity.

IMPROVE READING AND WRITING

Reading and writing are the cornerstones of learning in school. Some students don't like to read. They can't stay focused, or they struggle with vocabulary. Other students love to write songs, stories, and poems. However, they may have difficulty organizing an essay. Reading and writing assignments will get more complex as you move through school. It will pay off to improve your skills in these key areas.

BECOME AN ACTIVE READER

Some students think that studying is just reading the same material over and over. But when they get to class the next day, they can't really remember what they read. Their eyes looked at the words, but their brains were not engaged.

If you want to improve your reading and studying, learn to interact with the text. Think about why you are reading and what you want to get out of the book, article, or story. If you are reading a textbook, pay attention to headings, subheadings, graphs, and pictures. Turn the headings into questions. Challenge yourself to find the main idea of each section and answer the question. After reading a section, close your eyes and summarize it. This takes more time than just reading the chapter quickly. However, what you have read will make sense. You will likely not have to keep rereading the chapter to remember what was in it.

If you can't write in your book, use sticky notes to leave comments or questions in the book. Try to apply what you are reading to your own life. For example, environmental science concepts such as the water cycle might relate to problems in your own community. Or historical events such as the Civil War might have impacted your state. These strategies will help you understand not just the facts but also why they are important.

If you are reading a novel, try to connect with the characters. Think about what you would do in their place. Predict what you think they will do next. By becoming involved with your book, you will gain insight into the plot, theme, and motives. You will be able to figure out what the author's purpose is and how he or she achieves it. These critical thinking skills can be used in almost any subject.

USE THE WRITING PROCESS

When beginning to write, brainstorming techniques such as webbing, clustering, or concept mapping can help you develop

AVOIDING PLAGIARISM

Plagiarism is using other people's words and ideas without giving them credit. It is dishonest and against academic rules. Teachers are very good at spotting when you are using someone else's ideas or words. Here are some good ways to avoid plagiarism. First, write down all your sources as you take notes. Then, learn how to cite your sources. "In-text" citations go in parentheses after the sections you quote, paraphrase, or summarize. Bibliographical citations appear in the bibliography. A good rule to follow is that if you didn't know a fact before you started your research, you have to cite it. You can find style guides on the Internet that show the format and punctuation to use. Your teacher will let you know which style to follow. There are even online tools such as EasyBib (http://www.easybib.com) that will format bibliography entries for you; you just need to double-check to make sure all of the information is correct.

an idea. In these techniques, you write the main topic or theme in the center of the page. Branching out from the center, you quickly write down everything you can think of about the topic. Then you go back and find connections among your ideas.

When your main idea emerges, turn it into a topic or thesis sentence. The five "Ws"—the who, what, when, where, and why or how of your topic—can provide details for the body paragraphs. As you write your first draft, leave grammar and punctuation issues aside until the proofreading stage. You don't want to interrupt the flow of ideas while they are coming.

Try to get as much feedback as you can about your draft from friends, siblings, parents, and teachers, if possible. Many students do not like to revise after writing down their first ideas. However, editing and revising are among the most important stages of writing. If your paragraphs are disorganized or your main ideas lack support, you need to fix those problems. Also check to see if you have transitions from one paragraph to the next.

It's a good idea to create an outline before you begin writing. However, if you didn't create one then, you can do it at this point to be sure that the ideas in your piece are the ones you want to communicate.

The last stage is proofreading. A good strategy is to read your piece out loud to yourself so you can hear any mistakes. Using the grammar and spelling checks on a computer can also help you catch your errors.

USE A GRAPHIC ORGANIZER TO PLAN YOUR ESSAY

Organizing an essay can be difficult. Planning your essay with a graphic organizer before writing it can help. A visual method of organizing your thesis statement and body paragraphs is the "chicken foot" organizer (see facing page). A chicken has a long skinny leg with three long, flat claws at the end. Let's say you are trying to write an essay about why you might choose the military as a career. Your main idea, "I believe the military will be the best choice for a career," goes on the leg. Your three reasons why— "The military will be exciting," "I will serve my country," and "I can learn lifelong skills"—go on the claws. These reasons are your body paragraphs. Then take each reason and create a chicken foot for it. For example, put "I can learn lifelong skills" on a leg.

THE CHICKEN FOOT

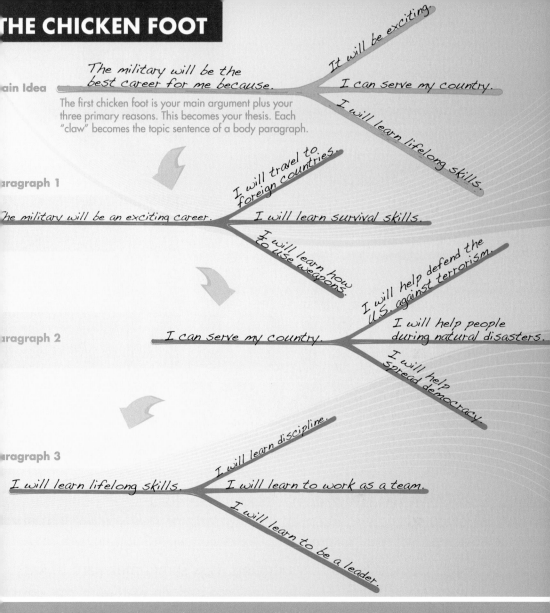

ain Idea — The military will be the best career for me because.

The first chicken foot is your main argument plus your three primary reasons. This becomes your thesis. Each "claw" becomes the topic sentence of a body paragraph.

It will be exciting.

I can serve my country.

I will learn lifelong skills.

aragraph 1 — The military will be an exciting career.

I will travel to foreign countries.

I will learn survival skills.

I will learn how to use weapons.

aragraph 2 — I can serve my country.

I will help defend the U.S. against terrorism.

I will help people during natural disasters.

I will help spread democracy.

aragraph 3 — I will learn lifelong skills.

I will learn discipline.

I will learn to work as a team.

I will learn to be a leader.

Despite its funny name, this graphic organizer will help you logically organize an essay with a thesis statement, topic sentences for your body paragraphs, and supporting details.

"I'll learn discipline," "I'll learn to work as a team," and "I'll learn to be a leader" go on each of the claws. These are the supporting details for your lifelong skills paragraph. After you create all of your chicken feet, you will have the perfect outline for your essay.

CONQUER MATH AND SCIENCE

o you find that science classes are your most difficult? Do you struggle to keep up in math and believe you are just not good at it? The STEM (science, technology, engineering, and math) classes can be challenging. It is sometimes hard to keep a positive attitude. However, anyone can do well with the right approach.

MASTERING MATH

Math is like playing an instrument, learning a foreign language, or becoming a fast runner. It needs daily practice. That is why it is so important to do your homework each day. Math is often sequential. You must thoroughly learn one step before going on to the next.

SOLVING WORD PROBLEMS

Do you find word problems in math confusing? Many students do. Here are some suggestions for solving them:

- Write down the information you are given.
- Write down what you are supposed to find.
- Translate English words into math procedures. For example, "is" means "equals." "Times" means "multiply."
- Find a similar non-word problem you can use as a model.
- Draw a picture, if possible.
- After you solve the problem, see if the answer makes common sense.

A math book is organized to help you understand the lessons. It presents the concepts and defines the new vocabulary words. Typically, each lesson gives you several examples, including at least one that applies the concept to the real world. When doing your homework, go back and find the book's example for each type of problem. Or look in your notes for the example your teacher explained in class. Substitute the numbers and variables in the homework for the ones in the example. Then follow the steps exactly.

Make sure your problems are neatly organized on your paper. Then, when you look at them later, you will still be able to follow what is going on. Showing all your work also helps the teacher figure out where you went wrong if you do get an incorrect answer.

It might help to do your homework with a classmate. He or she may have a different approach to a problem that helps you see

USING THE INTERNET

The Internet can be a great resource for projects and research papers. Some students, however, just Google their topics. Then they use the first Web sites that come up. Some Web sites will have current, accurate information, but others may have out-of-date or incorrect facts. You can trust your school library or public library's online databases. Some databases focus on science or history. Others are more general. For example, CQ Researcher and EBSCO's Kids Search collect articles about hundreds of topics from a wide variety of sources. Check with your school or public librarian because you may need a password to access the databases.

it in a new way. If it is difficult to meet with a friend, check out math videos on the Internet. YouTube has many short math videos that use animation. There are also online tutoring Web sites that can help you if you get stuck. Check the online resources on your local library's Web site or on Great Websites for Kids from the American Library Association (http://gws.ala.org).

MASTERING SCIENCE

Many students love science classes because they can do hands-on projects and experiments. The labs allow them to see how the organs work in an insect or what happens when chemicals are combined.

One challenge in science is all the new vocabulary. Many scientific words come from Latin or Greek. They share similar prefixes, suffixes, and roots. One strategy is to make flash cards to use to review. Or you can keep an ongoing glossary of new words.

When reading science textbooks, pay particular attention to the visuals on the page. They are essential to making sense of the information. You may have to keep going back and forth between reading the text and looking at a diagram or graph. Linking the words and the pictures in your mind will increase your understanding of the concepts.

The Internet has many interactive science Web sites. They can make physical and life science come alive. For example, you can learn about the principles of plate tectonics while watching an earthquake simulation. Connecting textbook concepts to exciting real or virtual events can deepen your understanding of and appreciation for science.

Some students complain that they will never use the concepts they learn in math and science classes. However, the problem-solving skills that you are developing will help you throughout your life.

USGS

This Dynamic Earth: the Story of Plate Tectonics

Online edition

Watching online simulations of scientific processes can help you understand them. Government agencies and major research institutions often create them to interest students in science.

MAKE A HOMEWORK PLAN

Are you spending hours and hours on homework each night? Do you wish you could get it done more efficiently and have more time for what you want to do? Here are some strategies that can help.

MAKE A REGULAR HOMEWORK SCHEDULE

Most teens have an energy cycle. For example, some students like to do their homework right after school when they can still remember the lessons. Other students need to chill out after school. Or they are busy with sports or school activities. They recharge during dinner and then attack their homework. Figure

CREATE A COMPUTER FILING SYSTEM

Take a tip from office professionals and organize your word processing documents on your home computer. Create a folder with your name on it on your hard drive. Inside that folder, create folders for each of your classes. You can drag and drop all of your documents from your computer desktop into the folders. If you work in your school's computer lab, you will need a way of transporting documents back and forth from home. An inexpensive flash drive works well. However, if you have access to the Internet both at home and at school, cloud computing works even better. Google Docs is an example of a cloud computing system that is easy to learn. All of your work will be available to you wherever you are. All you need is an Internet connection.

out when you have the greatest ability to focus and then stick to that schedule.

ATTACK HOMEWORK WITH A PLAN

A homework to-do list can be a lifeline for busy students. First, make a list of everything you have to do. Estimate how long each task will take. Then break long assignments or projects into shorter sections. Checking off the items as you do them will give you a sense of accomplishment.

Some students like to do the hardest assignments first, when they have the most energy. Others like to get all of the short, easy ones out of the way. Try doing your homework each way to see which one works the best for you.

Take a short break every thirty to forty-five minutes. Make some popcorn, go out and look at the stars, or play with your pet for a few minutes. But stay at the homework until it's done.

ORGANIZE A STUDY AREA

A study area at home is a must. Clean off the desk in your room, or find another quiet place with good lighting. Put binder paper, pens and pencils, a pencil sharpener, stapler, ruler, dictionary, and calculator all in one place. A bulletin board with a calendar you can write on will help you keep track of important dates and deadlines. You will be surprised at how quickly you can get your homework done when you have what you need.

Multitasking while doing homework is not a good idea. Contrary to what you may think, listening to music while studying

Staying focused while doing your homework will help you get it done faster and more accurately. Once it's done, you can relax and enjoy time with friends and family.

will not help you concentrate. A 2010 study at University of Wales Institute in Cardiff, United Kingdom, found that music interfered with memory tasks. Similarly, texting while doing homework can distract you and slow you down. It makes a lot more sense to work efficiently until you are finished. Then reward yourself with a video game, chatting with friends, or television.

10 GREAT QUESTIONS

1 HOW CAN I IMPROVE MY WRITING SKILLS?

2 WHAT CAN I DO TO HELP ME REMEMBER INFORMATION FOR TESTS?

3 HOW CAN I KEEP TRACK OF ALL MY BOOKS AND MATERIALS?

4 WHAT CAN I DO IF I'M BORED IN MY CLASSES?

5 WHAT CAN I DO IF A FRIEND IS THINKING OF DROPPING OUT OF SCHOOL?

6 HOW CAN I GET OVER MY ANXIETY ABOUT TAKING STANDARDIZED TESTS?

7 WHERE CAN I GET EXTRA HELP IN MY DIFFICULT CLASSES?

8 I'M OVERWHELMED BY THE AMOUNT OF HOMEWORK I GET. WHAT SHOULD I DO?

9 WHAT DO YOU THINK MY LEARNING STYLE IS, AND HOW CAN I USE IT TO HELP ME DO WELL?

10 WHAT SHOULD I DO IF I THINK I HAVE A LEARNING DISABILITY?

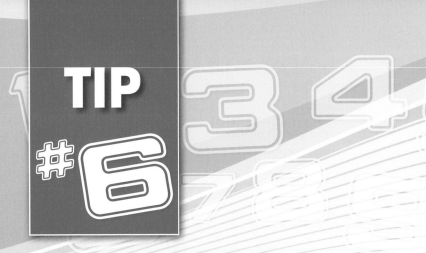

BECOME INVOLVED IN YOUR SCHOOL

E very school year you are faced with a vast array of sports, clubs, and outside organizations to join. It's fun to become involved with all of these activities. The benefits are endless. You meet new friends and learn new skills. You develop new interests outside of school. You learn to be a leader and to work as a team. But school and outside activities can also overwhelm you. They can distract you from your first priority, your classes. Good time management will allow you to maintain balance in your life.

ACTIVITIES TO CONSIDER

Sports are a traditional way to get involved. If you love a sport but can't make the team, ask if you can become a manager. Team managers help the team stay organized with rosters and equipment. Cheerleading and dance teams also provide opportunities to be part of sports events.

If you are not talented at sports but like competition, look into an Academic Olympics or Science Bowl organization. Members of these groups combine specialized knowledge with teamwork. They compete against other schools for state and national awards. Their events can be as exciting as basketball or tennis.

Clubs and activities, such as a robotics club, are a fun way to meet new friends and explore your interests. They can also help provide direction toward college and careers.

Foreign language clubs often plan trips to other countries to practice their language skills. Speech and debate clubs sharpen critical thinking and speaking for budding attorneys and politicians. Key Club service groups send you out to the community to do volunteer activities. Robotics, musical theater, Future Business Leaders of America, and Junior ROTC are all opportunities to learn leadership and cooperation. In addition you will have a lot of fun.

If you are shy, school clubs provide a smaller group to get to know. One student didn't find a club she wanted to join, so she started her own. She had always enjoyed origami and wanted to introduce it to her friends. Her math teacher agreed to be the

WORKING IN GROUPS

Many teachers, coaches, and club advisers ask students to work in groups because it teaches them important life lessons. A lot of work in the adult world is done in groups. Here are some suggestions for becoming a good team player in groups:

- First, contribute your ideas; don't force everyone else to make all the decisions.
- Make sure you understand all the instructions for the project by asking questions. Make a commitment to a quality project you can all be proud of.
- Politely let the other group members know if you disagree with something.
- Do your share of the project without being reminded. By stepping up and completing your part of the work, you will show that others can depend on you.
- Finally, communicate with your group members so you are aware of each other's progress and can coordinate the parts of the project that you need to do together.

adviser. The club made origami items as a fund-raiser for victims of the Japanese earthquake and tsunami in 2011.

MAINTAINING BALANCE

Be careful about committing yourself to too many activities. If you don't have enough downtime to relax, you may experience burnout. You may be so stressed that nothing will seem fun. Choose the activities you really enjoy and concentrate on those. You will remember your years participating in these activities as some of the best in your life.

TIP #7

MANAGE YOUR TIME

Unfortunately, when you learn to tell time, you don't necessarily learn how to manage it. You may have three weeks to do a school project. The next thing you know, you are staying up all night before the due date. Or, you may wake up one morning realizing that you have to be in two places at once. If you have trouble finding enough time to do everything you have to do plus everything you want to do, you need time management.

The most important part of time management is setting priorities. The short- and long-term goals you set for yourself at the beginning of the semester are the place to start. For example, say it is Sunday and you have a big history project due Monday. You haven't even started it yet. Friends call you with an invitation to go snowboarding. You are tempted to head for the slopes instead of working on your project. Although you may feel sad, your decision is a no-brainer if one of your short-term goals is a better grade in history. However, this conflict could have been avoided with better time management.

If you are like many students, you can find all kinds of ways to avoid doing schoolwork. Cell phones, iPods, and video games can easily lure you away from homework. Often, students think they do their best work at the last minute. Mostly, though, they admit that their best work comes as a result of thoughtful planning. This chapter will give you some tools for better managing your time.

TOOLS FOR TIME MANAGEMENT: THE PLANNER

Your planner can help you stay on top of your busy schedule. By using it to plan ahead, you can avoid a lot of stress in your life.

A planner is the single most important tool a busy student can use to manage time. A planner is a small notebook with daily, weekly, and monthly calendars. You can find good-looking ones in bookstores or office supply stores. Or you can make your own with downloaded pages from the Internet. The most useful academic planners allow you to see an entire week in a two-page open spread. They also have pages that show each month.

The more you use a planner, the easier it will become to remember to enter important due dates, school activities, and family events. Here are some tips for effective use of your planner:

- Write down tests, quizzes, and project due dates on the day they are announced. Then transfer the information to the due date or test date.
- For major papers or projects, subtract two days and make the earlier date your deadline. Then you have a cushion in case anything comes up.
- More teachers are posting homework schedules online. Still, compiling all of your different teachers' assignments in your planner will help you see the big picture.
- Include school, sports, community, religious, social, and family activities. Color code them so you can clearly see conflicts.
- Plan downtime for relaxation and fun.

A monthly calendar can allow you to see several weeks ahead. You can use the one found in your planner or post a large version above your homework space. Note important due dates and activities so you always have an idea of what is coming up.

PLANNING FOR LONG-TERM PROJECTS

Writing a research paper, working on a group project, or reading a novel for a report all need more than just a final due date.

TRACK YOUR USE OF TIME

Another strategy for time management is figuring out how your time is spent. Keeping a daily diary for a week can show you how you are actually spending your time. For example, one student wanted more time for photography. But there never seemed to be enough time to take pictures. His daily diary showed that he was spending several hours each day either hanging out with his girlfriend or talking to her on the phone. He quickly found a solution to his problem. His girlfriend agreed to be his photographer's assistant. Together they discovered interesting places to take pictures.

You need time for research, thought, collaboration, and hard work. You will be a lot more successful if you use the following strategies.

Break the paper or research project into separate steps. Examples are choosing a topic, finding resources, taking notes, writing or assembling, and proofreading. Give each step its own due date in your planner.

For reports on novels, assign yourself several chapters to read each week. Write them down in your planner. If you carry your book wherever you go, you can find unexpected pockets of time to read. Make sure you will finish the book early enough to have time to write the report.

Instead of a big, overwhelming project, you now have five or ten little jobs that you can attack one by one. You will feel a great deal of satisfaction as you cross off each job on your to-do list. And you will avoid the stress that builds up when you put off a project.

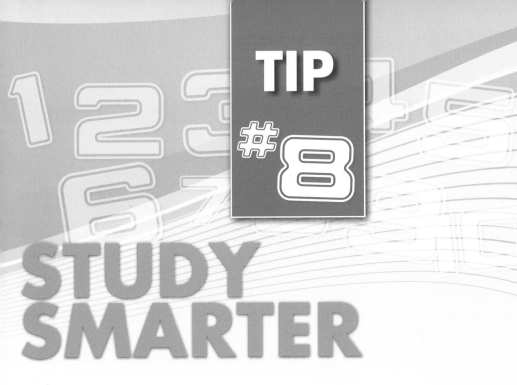

STUDY SMARTER

T eachers are often dismayed when they see their carefully organized lecture turn into a jumble of words on a student's paper. You can learn to take good notes. However, taking notes in class is only the beginning. Keeping them organized and actively reviewing them can make a huge difference in getting good grades on tests.

TAKING GOOD NOTES

Many teachers give out graphic organizers for taking notes. If your teachers don't, then you can make your own. The Cornell Method is a great system. On your binder paper, draw a vertical line about 2 inches (5.1 cm) from the left edge. Then draw a horizontal line about 1.5 inches (3.8 cm) from the bottom. As your teacher talks, write down the main ideas in the large space of the paper. Don't write in complete sentences.

Questions	Notes
What is a tsunami?	Tsunamis From Jap. word for "harbor wave."
How are tsunamis created?	Series of water waves caused by: earthquakes, volcanic eruptions, glaciers breaking apart, meteorite impacts, underwater nuclear explosions. Wave length is longer than normal sea waves. May first start as a rapid rising tide. Then waves come in a series, ranging from minutes to more than an hour between wave crests. They can cross entire oceans. In 1946 a 7.8 earthquake in Alaska generated a tsunami that hit Hilo in Hawaii with 46-ft. high surge.
Why are they so destructive?	Damage is caused by (1) A wall of water moving at high speed crashing onto land, (2) Water draining off the land carrying everything with it. In 1992 and 1993 over 2,000 were killed in Nicaragua, Indonesia, and Japan 2004 Indian Ocean was the most deadly one – killed over 230,000 in countries.
Where are some recent tsunamis?	In 2011 a 9.0 undersea earthquake near Japan created tsunami waves to 130 ft. high and covered 217 square miles. Caused nuclear meltdowns at Fukushima Power Plant, almost 16,000 deaths and over 3,000 missing.
How can residents protect themselves from tsunamis?	The Pacific Tsunami Warning System in Hawaii monitors seismic activity in the Pacific. 26 countries belong. There are identified evacuation centers on higher ground.

Summary

Tsunamis are a series of large tides and waves caused by large under ocean events such as volcanos and earthquakes. They are destructive for two reasons – a wall of water crashes onto the coast and then the water drains off, carrying everything with it. A 2004 earthquake-caused tsunami in the Indian Ocean killed over 230,000 and the 2011 tsunami in Japan killed almost 16,000 and destroyed 217 square miles. Early warning systems can help warn residents to head to high ground.

The Cornell note-taking method works well because it is based on brain science. It requires you to organize your notes into categories, which helps your brain remember the information

Do abbreviate when possible. Write down names, dates, and vocabulary words.

The most important part of the Cornell Method comes after the lecture. When you have time, use the left margin to organize the notes. Write headings and subheadings for the content. Also write questions that the various sections of the notes might answer. Use the bottom section under the notes to write a summary of that section. When it is time to study for a quiz or test, fold the paper so you can see only the questions you have written. You can quiz yourself to see what you remember. You can also review by reading your summaries.

PREPARING FOR TESTS

A 2008 study from the University of California–San Diego showed that cramming the night before a test is not effective. What does work is review over a longer period of time, such as a week. The brain uses sleep to put information from short-term memory into long-term memory. This same study also showed

KEEPING AN ORGANIZED BINDER

Managing the constant flow of notes, handouts, and papers passed out and turned in can be challenging. It is important to keep an organized binder. If your teachers don't require a certain format, try this. Buy or make four dividers with pockets. Label them class notes, long-term work, handouts, and graded work. Divider pockets can hold handouts that don't have holes. Zippered binder pouches can hold pencils, pens, highlighters, and calculators.

   If you often leave your homework sitting at home on your desk, do the work without taking it out of your binder. When you are finished with your homework, put the binder back in your backpack. Storing papers you don't need anymore in files at home will make finding what you do need easier.

that students who are sleepy are less productive than those who are alert. That is why sleeping before a test is a better idea than staying up all night studying. Use your planner to set up a study schedule for yourself. Write in all your major test dates. Then put in reminders to study in the weeks before the test.

An effective way to study vocabulary is to make flash cards. Write each word on a small index card. Write its definition or its English translation on the other side of the card. Quiz yourself frequently throughout the school year, adding cards as necessary. There are also free online flash card makers that can make studying fun.

If you have to memorize facts and procedures, make up an acronym. For example, the made-up word "IPMAP" can help you remember the stages of cell division: interphase, prophase, metaphase, anaphase, and telophase. "PEMDAS" is the order of operations in solving or evaluating math equations:

Setting up a study schedule so you can review material over time is a lot more effective than cramming the night before a test.

parentheses, exponents, multiplication, division, addition, and subtraction. You can also create a phrase to memorize the sequence, such as "Please excuse my dear Aunt Sally."

STRATEGIES FOR TAKING TESTS

When taking objective tests, such as tests using multiple-choice questions or matching, it makes sense to first do all the questions that you are positive you know. An item at the end of the test may provide an association that helps you recall a harder item at the beginning. You also won't run out of time, leaving some easy questions at the end unanswered. After quickly doing all of the easier questions, you have time to think about the more difficult ones.

For short-answer or essay questions, stop yourself from just writing everything you know about the topic. Underline the key words in the question that tell what is required for the answer. Words such as "explain," "analyze," and "discuss" ask you to go beyond summarizing the information on the topic. You will have to state why it is important. If your teacher allows, it is a good idea to do a "brain dump" before you start writing. This is a quick list of the main points you want to write about. Once you see your list, you can figure out how to arrange the main points. This way, you won't get to the end of your answer and realize that you forgot an essential detail.

MYTHS & FACTS

MYTH: MULTITASKING IS THE ONLY WAY TO GET EVERYTHING DONE.

FACT: MANY TEENS BELIEVE THEY CAN DO TWO THINGS AT ONCE. THEY SEND INSTANT MESSAGES WHILE DOING THEIR HOMEWORK. OR THEY DO RESEARCH ON THE WEB WHILE WATCHING TELEVISION. THOUGH TEENS BELIEVE THEY ARE DOING TWO OR THREE THINGS AT ONCE, THEY REALLY AREN'T. THEY ARE JUST SWITCHING THEIR ATTENTION BACK AND FORTH. EVERY TIME THEY SWITCH THEIR ATTENTION, THEY HAVE TO REMEMBER WHAT THEY WERE DOING BEFORE. THIS SLOWS THEM DOWN. ACCORDING TO A 2006 STUDY CONDUCTED BY RUSSELL POLDRACK AT THE UNIVERSITY OF CALIFORNIA–LOS ANGELES, MULTITASKING INTERFERES WITH LEARNING. DISTRACTIONS PREVENT INFORMATION FROM BEING STORED IN A PERSON'S LONG-TERM MEMORY. TRYING TO DO SEVERAL THINGS AT ONCE ALSO PROMPTS THE BODY TO RELEASE STRESS HORMONES, LEADING TO A LOSS OF SHORT-TERM MEMORY.

MYTH: CRAMMING IS AN EFFECTIVE WAY OF STUDYING.

FACT: SOME STUDENTS CRAM BEFORE EXAMS, THINKING IT IS AN EFFECTIVE METHOD. THEY WAIT UNTIL THE LAST MINUTE TO STUDY

AND THEN STAY UP LATE TO CRAM AS MUCH INFORMATION INTO THEIR BRAINS AS THEY CAN. RESEARCHERS HAVE LEARNED SOME THINGS ABOUT CRAMMING. ACCORDING TO HAL PASHLER, LEAD SCIENTIST IN A 2008 STUDY AT THE UNIVERSITY OF CALIFORNIA–SAN DIEGO, THE BRAIN DOESN'T LEARN WELL UNDER PRESSURE. YOU WON'T REMEMBER WHAT YOU HAVE READ IF YOU ARE STRESSED. PASHLER ALSO FOUND THAT TRYING TO STUDY IN ONE LONG SESSION ACTUALLY REDUCED RETENTION.

A BETTER IDEA IS TO USE YOUR PLANNER TO SPACE OUT YOUR STUDYING OVER AN EXTENDED PERIOD OF TIME. MOST STUDIES ON LEARNING SHOW THAT THE LONGER YOU CAN STUDY THE MATERIAL, THE MORE YOU WILL RETAIN. REVIEWING OVER WEEKS AND MONTHS WILL ENSURE THAT YOU WON'T FORGET WHAT YOU HAVE LEARNED. A 2007 STUDY AT BETH ISRAEL DEACONESS MEDICAL CENTER IN BOSTON FOUND THAT SLEEP AIDS LONG-TERM MEMORY. DURING SLEEP, THE BRAIN CONSOLIDATES THE DAY'S LEARNING.

MYTH: BOYS ARE BETTER AT MATH THAN GIRLS.

FACT: RESEARCH HAS NOT FOUND ANY DIFFERENCES BETWEEN THE SEXES WHEN IT COMES TO THEIR NATURAL ABILITY TO DO MATH. IN 2009, JANET HYDE, A PROFESSOR OF PSYCHOLOGY AT THE UNIVERSITY OF WISCONSIN–MADISON, ANALYZED STUDIES ON MATH ACHIEVEMENT FROM AROUND THE WORLD. SHE FOUND THAT IN MANY PLACES, GIRLS ARE DISCOURAGED FROM ADVANCING IN MATH. THEY HEAR A MESSAGE THAT SAYS THAT ONLY BOYS CAN GO INTO CAREERS INVOLVING MATH, SUCH AS ENGINEERING OR COMPUTER SCIENCE. HOWEVER, THERE ARE MANY WELL-PAYING OPPORTUNITIES FOR WOMEN IN THESE FIELDS.

COPE WITH STRESS

o you find yourself constantly stressed out? Many students feel as if their lives are a pressure cooker, ready to explode. They worry about trying to fit in or how they look. Tests, projects, and presentations pile up. Parents put pressure on them about grades or friends. They may face major stress from family conflict or illness. Learning about stress can help you cope with the stressful events in your life.

WHAT EXACTLY IS STRESS?

The stress response is the body's way of preparing for danger. When faced with a threat, our bodies are flooded with adrenaline (a stress hormone also known as epinephrine). Our muscles tense. We breathe faster and our hearts race. We become sharper and more focused. This is positive stress.

You may find that the sources of your stress are outside of you. Your classes are hard and demanding. Some older students are picking on you. Maybe your older sibling left home for college. Or one of your parents has lost his or her job.

Often, though, teens create their own internal stress. Some are perfectionists. They insist on getting 100 percent on

The teen years can be stressful. However, there are positive steps you can take to relieve school-related stress and feel more in control.

everything. Then they beat themselves up emotionally when they don't. Other teens are overconcerned with what others think of them. They stress out over how they look. Some create a lot of drama for themselves and those around them. They don't know how to control their emotions.

WHAT ARE THE EFFECTS OF STRESS?

Even when stressful events are over, some teens don't relax and rest. There are always new events coming up to gear up for. Some students pack their days with too many activities. They

AVOIDING DRUGS AND ALCOHOL

Students abuse drugs and alcohol for many reasons. They may have a hard time saying no to peer pressure. They may want to fit in with a particular group. They may also use these substances to try to escape from stress. But a temporary escape from problems doesn't solve them. In fact, abusing drugs and alcohol usually makes problems worse. A true sign of maturity is facing your problems instead of avoiding them. Asking for help when feeling overwhelmed is a great first step. In order to avoid peer pressure to drink or do drugs, a counselor can also teach you refusal skills. These are ways to say no to peers that allow you to maintain your self-respect. Getting involved in activities you enjoy such as sports or clubs can help you find friends who will support your efforts toward positive goals.

don't schedule enough time to just hang out and relax. Their muscles stay tense, even when they sleep. They feel exhausted all the time. Sometimes these students get headaches from the muscle tension. Or they abuse drugs or alcohol as a release. Eventually they burn out.

HOW CAN WE COPE BETTER WITH STRESS?

Psychologists tell us that events are not inherently stressful. Each one of us reacts to the same event in different ways. One student views a class skit as a fun way to learn French. A shy, less confident student sees that same skit as her worst nightmare. Stress comes from how you think about the event. Sometimes you can

Exercise is a great way to reduce stress. You relieve muscle tension, build strength and endurance, and have fun all at the same time.

reduce your stress by changing your attitude toward the stressful events in your life. Here are some ways to manage stress:

- Most people find that communicating about their problems helps them look at them in a new way. Writing in a journal can help you face your stressful thoughts. You can also tell your parents what is on your mind. For serious problems for which you don't want to approach your parents, your school counselor can be a valuable resource.
- Practice changing the negative chatter in your mind into more positive messages. Replace messages like "I can't do this" or "I hate doing this" with affirmations such as "I can do this" and "This will make me stronger and better."
- Exercise is great at relieving muscle tension. Shooting baskets, going for a run, or following a yoga video are all good ways to relax.

If you continue to feel stressed, reevaluate your schedule. You might need to look honestly at your commitments to see what needs to be cut. Try for a balance of school, social activities, time for hobbies, and enough time for sleep.

MAKE THE RIGHT CHOICES

Students today have so many choices to make. Some of them are easy. But even simple decisions like choosing what to wear to school each day can cause anxiety. How do you make the right choices? And how do you keep from becoming overwhelmed by all the choices you have to make? There is actually a clear answer to these questions. You make the choices that line up with the short- and long-term goals you have set for yourself. Keep your goals where you can see them frequently. Write them on your bathroom mirror or make them the wallpaper on your computer.

CHOICES ABOUT HEALTH

There is something addicting about junk food. Chips, soda, candy bars, and fries are often more appealing than fruit, yogurt, and salads. But you know the right way to feed your body so that you look good and feel good. When standing in front of a vending machine or in a convenience store, how do you make the right choice? You do it by thinking ahead. Instead of pulling out a dollar bill for the unhealthy processed food, you can pull out the apple you put in your backpack that morning. Instead of lining up for the fried food, you line up for the salad bar. This is because you have already decided to have a healthy diet.

Choosing healthy food will make you feel and look good. It will provide the nutrients and energy you need to be your best in everything you do.

Whether your goals are physical, such as getting in shape, or academic, such as getting better grades, you will be better equipped to achieve them by staying healthy. Eating right, challenging yourself physically, and getting enough sleep will pay off. They are like any other habits. The more you do them, the easier it gets. You will look better and feel better about yourself.

CHOICES ABOUT ATTITUDE

Here is an old saying: "If you can't change your circumstances, change your attitude." What does that mean? Some students, especially ones who do not do well in school, develop a negative attitude. They expect their teachers, their parents, or their friends to motivate them. Then they have someone to blame when they give up on a learning task or lose interest.

You can choose to see your classes as boring and irrelevant. Then they are, and you get little out of them. This results in bad grades. Instead, you can choose to see your classes as challenging and full of problems to be solved. You tap into your natural curiosity. You look for connections to your own life. The classes then become interesting. And you are inspired to do well.

Let's see how this choice to be motivated works. Let's say you think Shakespeare is old-fashioned, difficult, and boring. You can dread reading *Romeo and Juliet*, or you can change your attitude. You can approach the play with curiosity, wondering if a story that is so old can still relate to you. You can try to hear the music in Shakespeare's language. You might learn that some of your favorite actors and actresses have played roles from Shakespeare. Instead of being bored, you become

RESISTING BULLYING

Many students have been or know someone who has been bullied at school or online. Cyberbullying on social media Web sites such as Myspace or Facebook has increased dramatically. Being teased, threatened, or laughed at by peers can be devastating. Often, teachers and school administrators do not detect this kind of bullying. How can students who are targets of bullying fight back? The first step is to report the bullying to parents, teachers, counselors, or administrators. They can confront the bullies and discipline them for their behaviors. This will show the bullies that you will not tolerate their attacks.

interested. You find many connections between your life and the play. Reading it becomes a rewarding experience.

Changing how you view your classes can change your whole attitude toward school. When you approach your subjects with curiosity, they become much more interesting. Choosing to motivate yourself rather than relying on others is a true sign of maturity. As you make progress toward your goals, you will find that you are enjoying being successful in school.

GLOSSARY

ACRONYM A word formed from the first letters of all the words in a phrase.

ADRENALINE A hormone produced by the adrenal glands that helps the body meet physical or emotional stress; also known as epinephrine.

CLOUD COMPUTING System that allows a computer user to access and store computer applications on the Internet.

CLUSTERING A brainstorming method in which a writer quickly thinks of a central topic and then writes all of his or her associations with the topic.

COLLABORATION Working and cooperating as a group.

CONCEPT MAPPING A graphic way of visualizing relationships among several ideas or concepts.

CONSOLIDATE To strengthen and solidify.

CYBERBULLYING The use of the Internet or mobile devices to torment, threaten, harass, humiliate, embarrass, or otherwise target a person.

GRAPHIC ORGANIZER A visual representation of ideas, thoughts, concepts, or information, such as a Venn diagram. Graphic organizers can be used to brainstorm, structure writing projects, plan research, solve problems, take notes, or study information.

HEADING A title of a page, paragraph, section, or chapter.

INHERENT Belonging to someone or something as a part of its nature.

INVESTIGATIVE Given to inquiry, or discovering the answers to questions by gathering data.

MOTIVE The goal or object of a character's actions.

PLOT The main story line of a literary or dramatic work.

PREFIX A small part of a word placed before a root word to change its meaning.

PRIORITY Something given the highest importance.

RETENTION The act or power of remembering things.

ROOT The base word before prefixes or suffixes are attached.

SEQUENTIAL The following of one thing after another in an orderly way.

SUBHEADING A title for a smaller topic or subsection of text. A subheading comes after the main title.

SUFFIX A small part of a word placed after a root word to change its meaning.

THEME The main idea or purpose of a piece of art or literature.

VARIABLE A quantity that can have any one of a set of values; a symbol that represents such a quantity.

Academic Development Institute (ADI)
121 North Kickapoo Street
Lincoln, IL 62656
(217) 732-6462
Web site: http://www.adi.org
The Academic Development Institute (ADI) works with fami-
    lies, schools, and communities so that all children may
    become self-directed learners, avid readers, and
    responsible citizens, respecting themselves and those
    around them.

AdLit.org
WETA
2775 S. Quincy Street
Arlington, VA 22206
(703) 998-2600
Web site: http://www.adlit.org
AdLit.org is a national multimedia project offering informa-
    tion and resources to the parents and educators of
    adolescent readers and writers in grades four through
    twelve. AdLit.org is an educational initiative of WETA,
    the flagship public television and radio station in the
    nation's capital.

Association for Library Service to Children (ALSC)
American Library Association
50 East Huron
Chicago, IL 60611-2795
(800) 545-2433, ext. 2163
Web site: http://www.ala.org/alsc

The Association for Library Service to Children (ALSC) is the world's largest organization dedicated to the support and enhancement of library service to children. The organization sponsors Great Websites for Kids (http://gws.ala.org), a compilation of exemplary Web sites for children.

The College Board
45 Columbus Avenue
New York, NY 10023-6992
(212) 713-8000
Web site: http://www.collegeboard.org
The College Board is a not-for-profit organization committed to excellence and equity in education. The College Board helps students plan for, search, apply to, and pay for college.

Research Institute for Learning and Development
4 Militia Drive, Suite 20
Lexington, MA, 02421
(781) 861-3711
Web site: http://www.researchild.org
This not-for-profit educational and research organization is dedicated to helping all students become successful learners by empowering them to learn how to learn through effective executive function and learning strategies. The institute works to transform the lives of children, adolescents, and adults with learning difficulties, including dyslexia and attention-deficit/ hyperactivity disorder (ADHD).

Success Foundation
200 Swisher Road
Lake Dallas, TX 75065
(940) 497-9222
Web site: http://www.successfoundation.org
The Success Foundation provides youth with personal
　　　development resources to inspire them to reach new
　　　levels of achievement.

U.S. Department of Education
400 Maryland Avenue SW
Washington, DC 20202
(800) USA-LEARN [872-5327]
Web site: http://www.ed.gov
The mission of the Department of Education is to promote
　　　student achievement and preparation for global
　　　competitiveness by fostering educational excellence
　　　and ensuring equal access to education for all
　　　students.

UVic Learning Skills Program
Counselling Services, University of Victoria
P.O. Box 3025 STN CSC
Victoria, BC V8W 3P2
Canada
(250) 721-8341
Web site: http://coun.uvic.ca/learning/index.html
The University of Victoria's counseling center provides
　　　online resources for students who need help with
　　　learning and study skills.

Youth Canada
40 Promenade du Portage, Phase IV, 4D392
Mail Drop 403
Gatineau, QC K1A 0J9
Canada
Attn: Youth Operations Directorate
(800) O-CANADA [622-6232]
Web site: http://www.youth.gc.ca
This one-stop resource center for Canadian youth contains
    information on education, employment, health, careers,
    and finance.

WEB SITES

Due to the changing nature of Internet links, Rosen Publishing
has developed an online list of Web sites related to the
subject of this book. This site is updated regularly. Please use
this link to access the list:

http://www.rosenlinks.com/top10/schl

FOR FURTHER READING

Armstrong, William. *Study Is Hard Work.* 2nd ed. Boston, MA: David R. Godine, 1995.

Crossman, Anne. *Study Smart, Study Less: Earn Better Grades and Higher Test Scores, Learn Study Habits That Get Fast Results, Discover Your Study Persona.* Berkeley, CA: Ten Speed Press, 2011.

Fox, Janet S., and Pamela Espeland. *Get Organized Without Losing It.* Minneapolis, MN: Free Spirit Publishing, 2006.

Fry, Ronald W. *How to Study.* 7th ed. Boston, MA: Cengage Learning, 2012.

Green, Julie. *Super Smart Information Strategies: Write It Down* (Information Explorer). Ann Arbor, MI: Cherry Lake Publishing, 2010.

Monahan, Chris. *The Everything Guide to Algebra: A Step-by-Step Guide to the Basics of Algebra—in Plain English!* Avon, MA: Adams Media, 2011.

Moss, Samantha, and Lesley Schwartz. *Where's My Stuff? The Ultimate Teen Organizing Guide.* San Francisco, CA: Zest Books, 2007.

Muchnick, Cynthia Clumeck. *The Everything Guide to Study Skills: Strategies, Tips, and Tools You Need to Succeed in School!* Avon, MA: F+W Media, 2011.

Naik, Anita. *Beat Stress! The Exam Handbook* (Really Useful Handbooks). New York, NY: Crabtree Publishing, 2009.

O'Connor, Frances. *Frequently Asked Questions About Academic Anxiety* (FAQ: Teen Life). New York, NY: Rosen Publishing, 2007.

Paul, Kevin. *Study Smarter, Not Harder.* 3rd ed. North Vancouver, BC: Self-Counsel Press, 2009.

Phipps, Tessa. *Study for Success* (Life Skills). Chicago, IL: Heinemann Library, 2009.

Piscitelli, Stephen. *Study Skills: Do I Really Need This Stuff?* 3rd ed. Boston, MA: Pearson/Allyn and Bacon, 2013.

Robinson, Matthew. *Making Smart Choices About Time Management* (Making Smart Choices). New York, NY: Rosen Central, 2008.

Somervill, Barbara A. *Studying and Tests* (School Projects Survival Guides). Chicago, IL: Heinemann Library, 2009.

Somervill, Barbara A. *Written Reports* (School Projects Survival Guides). Chicago, IL: Heinemann Library, 2009.

Stern, Judith M., Uzi Ben-Ami, and Carl Pearce. *Many Ways to Learn: A Kid's Guide to LD*. Washington, DC: Magination Press, 2011.

Warner-Prokos, Luann, Tami Pleasanton, and Elizabeth Mulligan. *Study Skills Tool Kit*. Delray Beach, FL: Palm Tree Educational Press, 2008.

Allen, Laura. "Cramming: Not a Long-Term Study Strategy." *Popular Science*, November 20, 2008. Retrieved October 1, 2011 (http://www.popsci.com/scitech/article/2008-11/cramming-not-long-term-study-strategy).

Association for Psychological Science. "Back to School: Cramming Doesn't Work in the Long Term." August 29, 2007. Retrieved October 20, 2011 (http://www.psychologicalscience.org/media/releases/2007/rohrer.cfm).

Beth Israel Deaconess Medical Center. "To Understand the Big Picture, Give It Time—and Sleep." EurekAlert.org, April 20, 2007. Retrieved October 6, 2011 (http://www.eurekalert.org/pub_releases/2007-04/bidm-tut042007.php).

Bryner, Jeanna. "Girls Get Math: It's Culture That's Skewed." LiveScience.com, June 1, 2009. Retrieved December 12, 2011 (http://www.livescience.com/5482-girls-math-culture-skewed.html).

Burke, Jim. *ACCESSing School: Teaching Struggling Readers to Achieve Academic and Personal Success*. Portsmouth, NH: Heinemann, 2005.

Burke, Jim. *School Smarts: The Four Cs of Academic Success*. Portsmouth, NH: Heinemann, 2004.

Conner, Jerusha, Denise Pope, and Mollie Galloway. "Success with Less Stress." *Educational Leadership*, vol. 67, December 2009/January 2010, pp. 54–58.

Cushman, Kathleen. *Fires in the Mind: What Kids Can Tell Us About Motivation and Mastery*. San Francisco, CA: Jossey-Bass, 2010.

Downing, Skip. *On Course: Strategies for Creating Success in College and in Life.* 5th ed. Boston, MA: Houghton Mifflin, 2008.

Goldberg, Donna, and Jennifer Zwiebel. *The Organized Student: Teaching Children the Skills for Success in School and Beyond.* New York, NY: Simon & Schuster, 2005.

Goodwin, Bryan. "Bullying Is Common—and Subtle." *Educational Leadership*, vol. 69, September 2011, pp. 82–84.

Gorman, Christine. "The Brain: 6 Lessons for Handling Stress." *Time*, January 19, 2007. Retrieved September 19, 2011 (http://www.time.com/time/magazine/article/0,9171,1580401,00.html).

Hippie, Deana. *Note-Taking Made Easy: Strategies & Scaffolded Lessons for Helping All Students Take Effective Notes, Summarize, and Learn the Content They Need to Know.* New York, NY: Scholastic, 2010.

Medina, John. *Brain Rules: 12 Principles for Surviving and Thriving at Work, Home, and School.* Seattle, WA: Pear Press, 2008.

Neihart, Maureen. *Peak Performance for Smart Kids: Strategies and Tips for Ensuring School Success.* Waco, TX: Prufrock Press, 2008.

Richardson, Judy S., Valerie J. Robnolt, and Joan A. Rhodes. "A History of Study Skills: Not Hot, But Not Forgotten." *Reading Improvement*, vol. 47, no. 2, 2010, pp. 111–123.

Rosen, Christine. "The Myth of Multitasking." *The New Atlantis*, Spring 2008. Retrieved August 29, 2011

(http://www.thenewatlantis.com/publications/
the-myth-of-multitasking).

Rutgers University. "Direct Evidence of Role of Sleep in Memory Formation Is Uncovered." ScienceDaily.com, September 15, 2009. Retrieved October 2, 2011 (http://www.sciencedaily.com/releases/2009/09/090915174506.htm).

Spinks, Sarah. "Inside the Teenage Brain." *Frontline*. PBS. WGBH Educational Foundation, January 2002. Retrieved October 2011 (http://www.pbs.org/wgbh/pages/frontline/shows/teenbrain).

Strong, Richard W., Harvey F. Silver, Matthew J. Perini, and Gregory M. Tuculescu. *Reading for Academic Success: Powerful Strategies for Struggling, Average, and Advanced Readers, Grades 7–12*. Thousand Oaks, CA: Corwin, 2002.

Wagner, Petra, Barbara Schober, and Christiane Spiel. "Time Investment and Time Management: An Analysis of Time Students Spend Working at Home for School." *Educational Research & Evaluation*, vol. 14, no. 2, 2008, pp. 139–153.

Wiley-Blackwell. "Background Music Can Impair Performance, Cites New Study." ScienceDaily.com, July 27, 2010. Retrieved December 13, 2011 (http://www.sciencedaily.com/releases/2010/07/100727112521.htm).

Zins, Joseph, Roger P. Weissberg, Margaret C. Want, and Herbert J. Walberg, eds. *Building Academic Success on Social and Emotional Learning: What Does Research Say?* New York, NY: Teachers College Press, 2004.

INDEX

ABOUT THE AUTHOR

Susan Henneberg has been inspiring high school and community college students to achieve their personal and academic goals for over thirty years. She originated the tutoring center and study skills programs at Truckee Meadows Community College and assisted in the creation of the Academic Success program at TMCC High School in Reno, Nevada. With her husband, Gene, she has raised three accomplished daughters. She currently teaches high school English, U.S. history, and Academic Success.

PHOTO CREDITS

Cover © istockphoto.com/Sean Locke; p. 5 Digital Vision/Thinkstock; p. 7 Jupiterimages/Goodshoot/Getty Images/Thinkstock; p. 11 © istockphoto.com/LeggNet; p. 12 © istockphoto.com/monkeybusiness; p. 14 © Michael Newman/PhotoEdit; p. 23 USGS.gov; p. 26 Ryan McVay/Photodisc/Thinkstock; p. 29 Beach Cities Robotics; p. 32 © Spencer Grant/PhotoEdit; p. 38 © istockphoto.com/Bowdenimages; p. 43 Stockbyte/Thinkstock; p. 45 IT Stock Free/Polka Dot/Thinkstock; p. 48 Hemera/Thinkstock; back cover & interior graphic Shutterstock/phyZick.

Designer: Nicole Russo; Editor: Andrea Sclarow Paskoff; Photo Researcher: Marty Levick